Gabriella
Ella
teea

The Brick Testament

The Ten Commandments

Library of Congress Cataloging in Publication Number: 2004109554

ISBN: 1-59474-044-5

Printed in Singapore

Typeset in Agincourt, Edwardian Medium, and Goudy

Designed by Andrea Stephany

Distributed in North America by Chronicle Books
85 Second Street
San Francisco, CA 94105

10 9 8 7 6 5 4 3 2 1

Quirk Books
215 Church Street
Philadelphia, PA 19106
www.quirkbooks.com

The Brick Testament

The Ten Commandments

Retold and Illustrated by Brendan Powell Smith

QUIRK BOOKS

PHILADELPHIA

Contents

Introduction

Illustrating the Bible in LEGO® was not my first career choice. And being an adult who makes a living playing with a children's toy has sometimes earned me the ridicule of my peers. But I would not think for a second of going back to my old nine-to-five job. Why? It is simple. Because when God tells you to do something, you do it.

This is one of the greatest lessons to be learned from the story of Moses and the Ten Commandments. And it is as true today as it was in ancient Egypt. We all struggle to do what God has commanded of us, even when it strikes us as preposterous, outlandish, or unthinkable.

We all are like Moses, and so, in some sense, this is the story of us all . . .

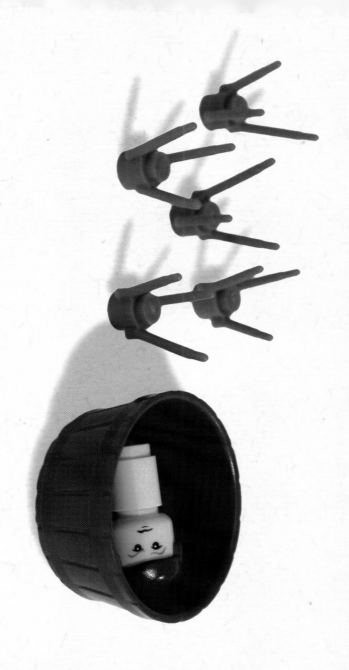

Moses Is Born

The Israelites came to Egypt and were fruitful and increased greatly in number. Eventually they became so numerous that the land was full of them.

Ex 1:1, 7

A new king came to power in Egypt who said to his people,
"The Israelites are becoming more numerous and powerful than us."

Ex 1:8–9

"We must deal with them wisely, or they will keep increasing in number, and if a war breaks out, they might join our enemies and drive us from the land."

Ex 1:10

And so the Egyptians put taskmasters over the Israelites
to wear them down with forced labor.

Ex 1:11

13

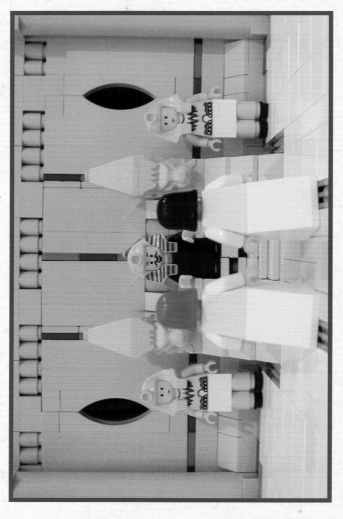

The king of Egypt spoke to the Hebrew midwives Shifrah and Puah and said,
"When you assist the Hebrew women in childbirth, examine the child.
If it is a boy, kill him. If it is a girl, allow her to live."

Ex 1:15–16

14

But the midwives feared God and did not obey the orders of the king of Egypt. They allowed the boys to live.

Ex 1:17

Then the king of Egypt summoned the midwives and said,
"Why have you allowed the boys to live?
Throw every boy who is born into the Nile!"

Ex 1:18, 22

16

Now a man and a woman from the tribe of Levi had been married.

And the woman became pregnant and gave birth to a son.

Ex 2:1–2

When she saw that he was a fine child, she kept him hidden for three months.

Ex 2:2

18

When she could no longer hide him, she took a papyrus basket, coated it with slime and pitch, and put the child in it, laying it in the reeds by the bank of the Nile river.

Ex 2:3

19

The child's sister stood a distance away to see what would happen to him.

Ex 2:4

Then Pharaoh's daughter went to bathe in the Nile while her maids walked alongside the river.

Ex 2:5

And there among the reeds she saw the basket.

Ex 2:5

Opening the basket, she found that the baby was crying.
She felt pity for it and said, "This is one of the Hebrews' babies."

Ex 2:6

Then the child's sister said,
"Shall I go and get a Hebrew woman to nurse the child for you?"
"Go," Pharaoh's daughter said to her.

Ex 2:7–8

23

So the young girl went and got the child's own mother.

Ex 2:8

"Take this child," Pharaoh's daughter said to her, "and I shall pay you to nurse him for me."

Ex 2:9

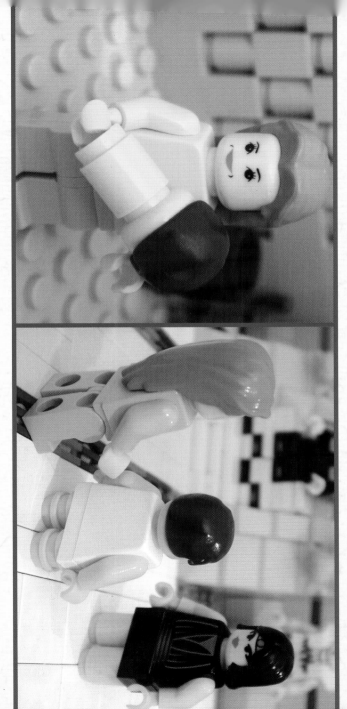

So the woman took the child and nursed him.

Ex 2:9

And when the child was grown,
she brought him to Pharaoh's daughter,
and he became her adopted son.

Ex 2:10

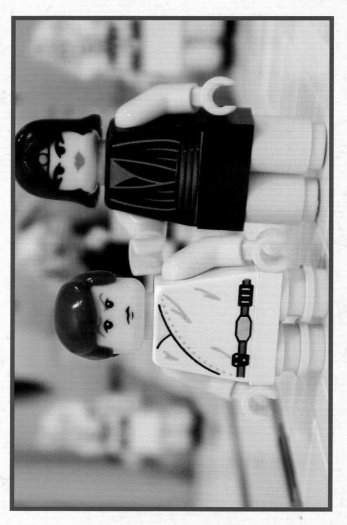

She named him Moses.

"Because," she said, "I drew him out of the water."

Ex 2:10

The End

Moses Commits Murder

One day when Moses had grown up, he went out to see his own people.

Ex 2:11

28

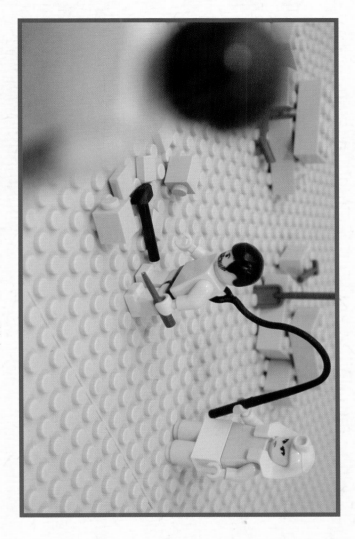

While watching their forced labor,
he saw an Egyptian striking a Hebrew, one of his people.

Ex 2:11

Moses looked this way and that and saw that there was no one watching.

Ex 2:12

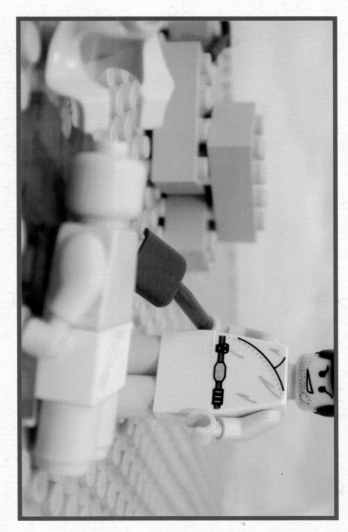

Then he killed the Egyptian.

Ex 2:12

31

And hid the body in the sand.

Ex 2:12

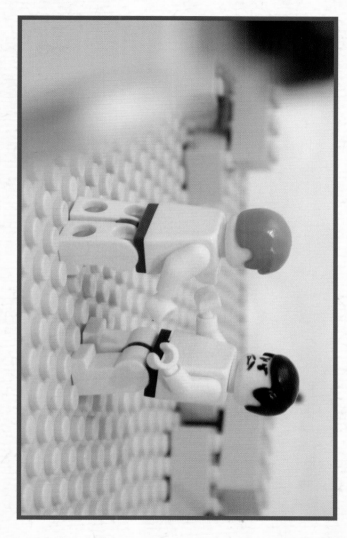

Moses went out the next day and came across two Hebrew men fighting.

Ex 2:13

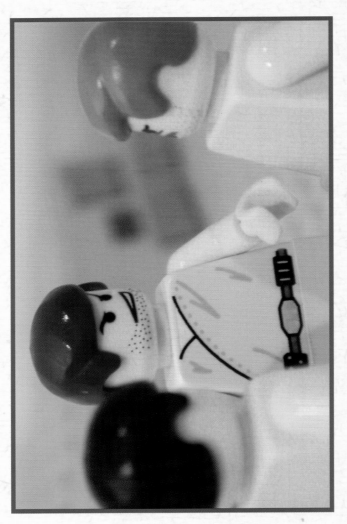

He said to the man who was in the wrong,
"Why are you hitting one of your own people?"
Ex 2:13

34

The man replied, "Who made you a ruler and judge over us?
Do you plan to kill me, as you killed the Egyptian?"

Ex 2:14

Moses was afraid, thinking, "Surely this matter has become known."

Ex 2:14

36

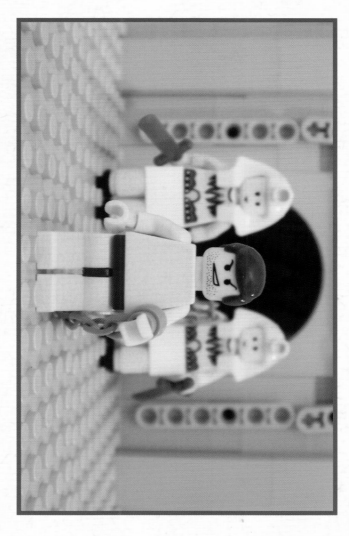

When Pharaoh heard of this incident, he sought to have Moses killed.

Ex 2:15

But Moses fled from Pharaoh.

Ex 2:15

The End

Moses Marries a Midianite

Moses fled from Pharaoh to the land of Midian.
As Moses sat by a well, the seven daughters of a Midianite priest
came to draw water for their father's flock.

Ex 2:16

Then some shepherds came along
and drove them away.

Ex 2:17

But Moses rose up to defend the sisters.

Ex 2:17

And he watered their flock.

Ex 2:17

When they returned to their father he said to them,
"Why did you just leave the man there?
Invite him to eat a meal with us!"

Ex 2:18, 2:20

Moses agreed to stay with the man,
and he gave Moses his daughter Zipporah in marriage.

Ex 2:21

43

Zipporah gave birth to a son, and Moses named him Gershom.
"Because," he said, "I am a stranger in a foreign land."

Ex 2:22

The End

44

The Burning Bush

After a great many years, the king of Egypt died.

Ex 2:23

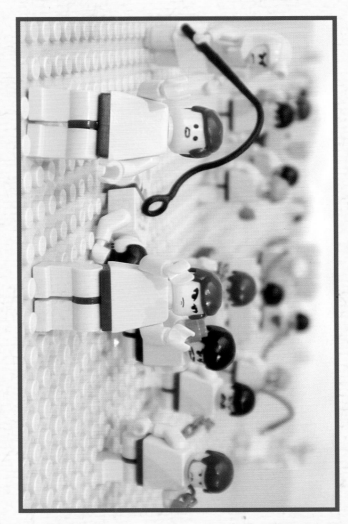

Groaning in their slavery, the Israelites cried out for help.

Ex 2:23

47

God heard their groaning and remembered his covenant with Abraham, with Isaac, and with Jacob.

Ex 2:24

Now Moses was tending the flock of his father-in-law, Jethro, the priest of Midian, and he led it to the far side of the desert and came to the mountain of God.

Ex 3:1

49

Moses looked and saw a bush blazing with fire, and yet the bush was not being burnt up.

Ex 3:2

50

God called to him from the middle of the bush,
"I am the God of your father, the God of Abraham, the God of Isaac,
and the God of Jacob."

Ex 3:4, 6

51

At this, Moses hid his face, for he was afraid to look at God.

Ex 3:6

52

God then said, "Go to the king of Egypt and say to him,
'Let us go and make a three-day journey into the desert
to offer sacrifices to our God.'"

Ex 3:7, 18

"But I will make Pharaoh stubborn," said God. "Then I will display my might by striking down the Egyptians with many miraculous deeds."

Ex 7:3, 3:20

Moses said to God, "Please, my Lord,
I have never been an eloquent man, for I speak slowly and awkwardly.
Please, my Lord, send anyone else you choose!"

Ex 4:10, 13

55

At this, God became angry with Moses and said,
"What about your brother, Aaron? I know that he is a good speaker.
He will speak to the people for you, acting as your mouthpiece."

Ex 4:14, 16

The End

56

The Staff of Aaron

Moses and Aaron went to Pharaoh, doing as God had ordered. Moses was eighty years old and Aaron was eighty-three when they spoke to Pharaoh.

Ex 7:7, 10

They said to Pharaoh, "This is what the God of Israel says:
'Let my people go, so that they may celebrate a feast to me in the desert.'"

Ex 5:1, 3

59

"Who is the God of Israel, for me to obey what he says?" said Pharaoh.
"I know nothing of the God of Israel and will not let the Israelites go."

Ex 5:2

Then Aaron threw his staff down in front of Pharaoh, and it became a snake.

Ex 7:10

Then Pharaoh called for the wise men and the sorcerers,
and they used their magic to do the same.
Each one threw down his staff, and they became snakes.

Ex 7:11–12

62

But Aaron's staff swallowed up theirs.

Ex 7:12

Yet Pharaoh became stubborn,
and he did not to listen to them, as God had foretold.

Ex 7:13

The End

The Ten Plagues

God then said to Moses, "Now you will see what I will do to Pharaoh. I have made him stubborn so that you may tell your children and grandchildren how I made fools of the Egyptians. Go to Pharaoh in the morning as he comes to the Nile's edge."

Ex 6:1, 10:1–2, 7:15

So Moses and Aaron did just as God had ordered.
Aaron raised up his staff in the sight of Pharaoh and struck the waters of the river.

Ex 7:20

67

And all the water that was in the Nile became blood.

Ex 7:20

68

The fish in the Nile died, and the river stank.

Ex 7:21

There was blood throughout all of Egypt,
and the Egyptians could not drink the water.

Ex 7:21

They all dug holes along the banks of the Nile,
searching for drinking water.

Ex 7:24

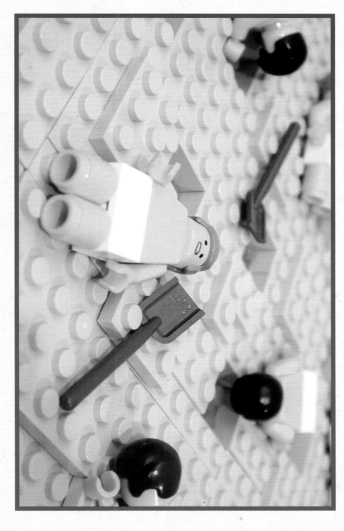

And seven days went by after God struck the river.

Ex 7:25

71

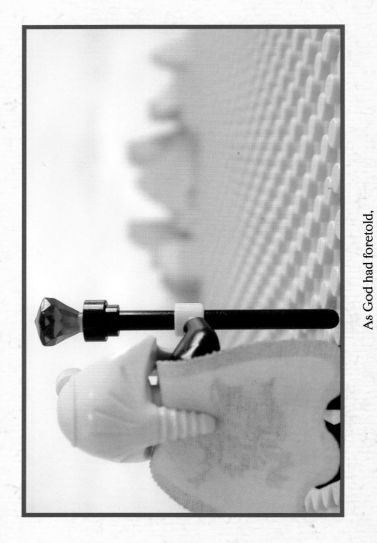

As God had foretold,
Pharaoh remained stubborn and did not listen to Moses and Aaron.
He turned away and went back to his palace.

Ex 7:22–23

Then Aaron extended his hand over the waters of Egypt, and frogs came up and covered the land.

Ex 8:6

They went into Pharaoh's palace.

Ex 8:3

And into the houses of his people.

Ex 8:3

And into their ovens and their kneading bowls.

Ex 8:3

But God made Pharaoh stubborn, and he did not listen to Moses and Aaron.

Ex 9:12, 8:15

So Aaron stretched out his hand with his staff and struck the dust of the earth.

Ex 8:17

And all the dust of the earth turned into mosquitoes throughout the land of Egypt. There were mosquitoes on people and on the animals.

Ex 8:17

But Pharaoh remained stubborn, as God had foretold, and did not listen to them.

Ex 8:19

Then God sent swarms of beetles against the Egyptians.
They went into Pharaoh's palace.

Ex 8:21, 24

And into the houses of his servants and his officials.

Ex 8:24

The whole land was ruined by the beetles, except the region of Goshen, where the Israelites were living. There were no beetles there.

Ex 8:24, 22

But Pharaoh became stubborn this time, too, and did not let the people go.

Ex 8:32

The next day, God struck the Egyptians' livestock in the fields with a terrible plague. All the livestock died—the horses, the donkeys, the camels, the oxen, the sheep, and the goats.

Ex 9:2–3, 6

But Pharaoh remained stubborn and did not let the people go.

Ex 9:7

God then said to Moses and Aaron, "Take handfuls of ashes from the furnace, and have Moses throw them in the air in sight of Pharaoh. They will become a fine dust over the whole of Egypt and cause festering boils on people and animals."

Ex 9:8–9

87

So they took ashes from the furnace and stood in front of Pharaoh, and Moses threw them in the air.

Ex 9:10

And on people and on animals they caused festering boils.

Ex 9:10

89

Then Moses extended his staff toward the sky.

Ex 9:23

And God sent hail that struck down anything
that was in the fields, both people and animals.

Ex 9:23, 25

It destroyed everything that grows in the fields
and broke all the trees.

Ex 9:25

But when Pharaoh saw that the hail had stopped,
he and his officials became stubborn again, as God had foretold,
and he did not let the Israelites go.

Ex 9:34–35

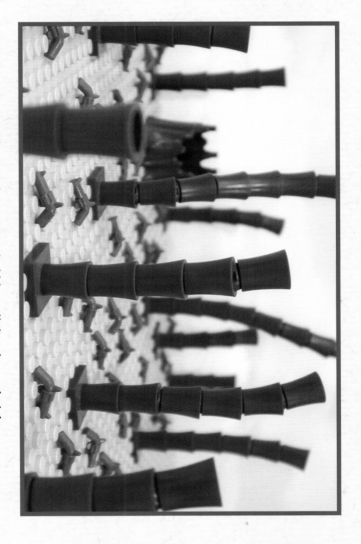

God then made an east wind blow all that day and night,
and by morning it had brought the locusts. They covered the surface of the land
and devoured any vegetation that the hail had left behind.

Ex 10:13–15

93

Then Moses extended his hand toward the sky.

Ex 10:22

But God made Pharaoh stubborn,
and he did not let the Israelites go.

Ex 10:20

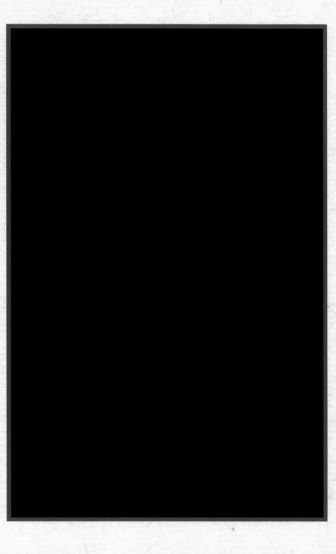

And there was thick darkness over all of Egypt for three days. No one could see one another or move about for three days.

Ex 10:22–23

God then said to Moses, "I shall bring one more plague on Pharaoh and Egypt. After that he will let you leave this place."

Ex 11:1

"Tell the whole community of Israel that each man must take an animal for his family, a one-year-old male without any blemishes, either a sheep or a goat."

Ex 12:1, 3–5

97

"You shall slaughter it at twilight."
Ex 12:6

"Then put some of the blood on the sides and top
of the doorframe of the houses where it will be eaten."
Ex 12:7

98

"I shall go throughout Egypt that night and kill the firstborn of all the people and animals, but when I see the blood, I shall pass over you, so you will not be destroyed."

Ex 12:12–13

99

And so at midnight God killed all the firstborn in the land of Egypt.

Ex 12:29

100

From the firstborn of Pharaoh . . .

Ex 12:29

. . . to the firstborn prisoner in the dungeon.

Ex 12:29

And Pharaoh woke up in the night his servants and all the Egyptians.

And there was a great wailing in Egypt,

for there was not a house without someone who was dead.

Ex 12:30

103

Pharaoh summoned Moses and Aaron when it was still night and said, "Rise! Get out from among my people, you and the Israelites! Go and worship the God of Israel as you have asked!"

Ex 12:31–32

The End

104

The Parting of the Red Sea

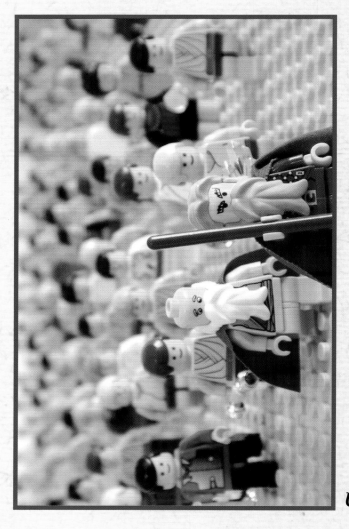

The Israelites traveled out of Egypt on foot, about six hundred thousand men strong, plus their families. The length of time that the Israelites had lived in Egypt was four hundred and thirty years.

Ex 12:37, 40

God spoke to Moses and said,
"I shall make Pharaoh stubborn, and he will pursue the Israelites.
I shall gain glory for myself at the expense of Pharaoh and his army."

Ex 14:1, 4

107

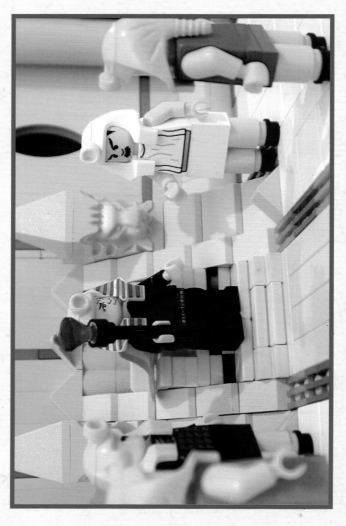

When Pharaoh was told that the Israelites had fled,
he and his officials changed their minds, saying, "What have we done,
releasing Israel from their service to us?"

Ex 14:5

So Pharaoh prepared his army, taking six hundred of his best chariots, plus all the other chariots in Egypt, with officers in each one.

Ex 14:6–7

109

God made Pharaoh stubborn,
and he pursued the Israelites and caught up with them.

Ex 14:8–9

As Pharaoh approached,
the Israelites looked up and saw the Egyptians in pursuit of them.
The Israelites were terrified and cried out to God.

Ex 14:10

And they said to Moses, "Did Egypt lack graves
that you had to lead us out into the desert to die?
'Leave us alone,' we told you,
'We would rather serve the Egyptians than die in the desert!'"

Ex 14:11–12

112

Moses said to the people, "Do not be afraid.
Stand firm, and you will see how God will save you today.
God will do the fighting for you, just keep silent."

Ex 14:13–14

God then said to Moses, "Stretch out your hand over the sea and divide it.
The Israelites will walk through the sea on dry land,
and I will make the Egyptians so stubborn that they will follow you."

Ex 14:15–17

114

Then Moses extended his hand out over the sea.

Ex 14:21

And God caused the sea to be driven back with a strong easterly wind, making the sea into dry land. And so the waters were divided.

Ex 14:21

The Israelites walked on dry land through the middle of the sea, with walls of water to their right and to their left.

Ex 14:22

The Egyptians pursued them. All Pharaoh's horses, chariots, and horsemen went into the middle of the sea after them.

Ex 14:23

But God threw the Egyptian army into confusion.

Ex 14:24

And he jammed their wheels so that the Egyptians shouted,
"Let us flee, for the God of Israel is fighting for them!"

Ex 14:25

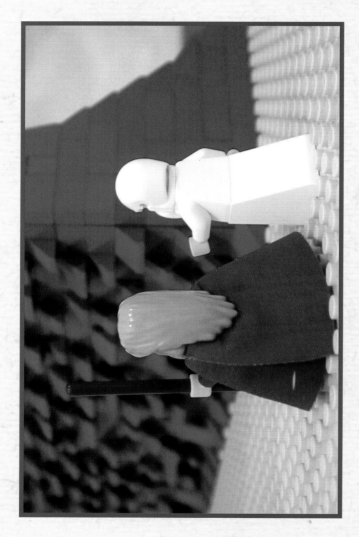

Then God said to Moses, "Extend your hand out over the sea
so that the waters will flow back on the Egyptians."

Ex 14:26

So Moses extended his hand out over the sea, and the sea returned to its place.

Ex 14:27

121

The Egyptians were trying to flee when God overthrew them in the middle of the sea. The waters came down over all the chariots and the horsemen and all of Pharaoh's army. Not a single one of them survived.

Ex 14:27–28

The Israelites saw the dead Egyptians on the seashore.

Ex 14:30

123

When Israel saw the great power that God had brought against the Egyptians, the people feared God and put their faith in Moses, his servant.

Ex 14:31

The End

124

The Ten Commandments

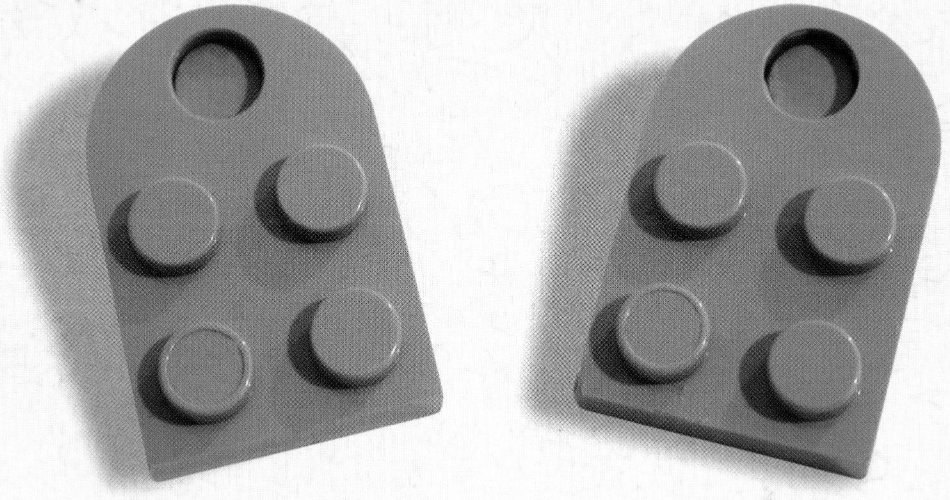

Three months after leaving Egypt, the Israelites came to the desert of Sinai. There they pitched camp, facing the mountain.

Ex 19:1–2

126

God then said to Moses, "I shall come to you in a thick cloud so that the people will hear when I speak to you. God will descend in sight of all the people on Mount Sinai."

Ex 19:9, 11

In the morning three days later, there was thunder, lightning, and a loud blast from a horn. Moses led the people to meet God, taking their place at the bottom of the mountain.

Ex 19:16–17

The horn grew louder and louder, and God descended on Mount Sinai. Then he called Moses to the top of the mountain, and Moses went up.

Ex 19:19–20

God then said to Moses, "Go back down and warn the people not to force their way through to look at God, or many of them will perish. God may send destruction against them!"

Ex 19:21–22

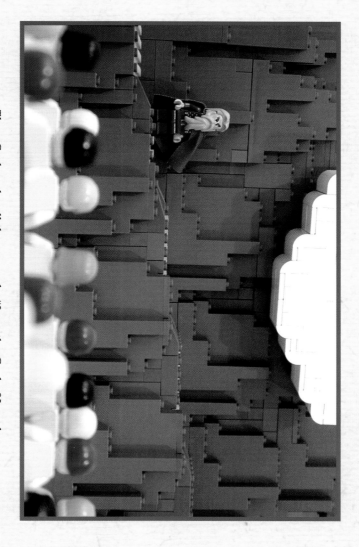

Then God spoke all these words: "I am the God of Israel.
You shall have no other gods before me.
Anyone who sacrifices to any other gods must be utterly destroyed."

Ex 20:1–3, 22:20

"You shall not make yourself a carved image or any likeness of anything in the heavens above, or on earth beneath, or in the waters below the earth."

Ex 20:4

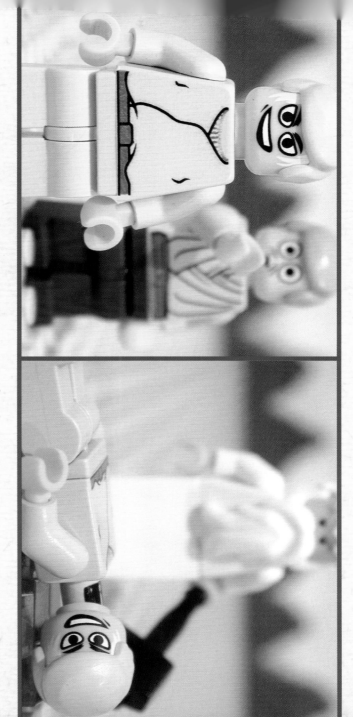

"You shall not misuse the name of God,
for God will not leave unpunished anyone who misuses his name."

Ex 20:7

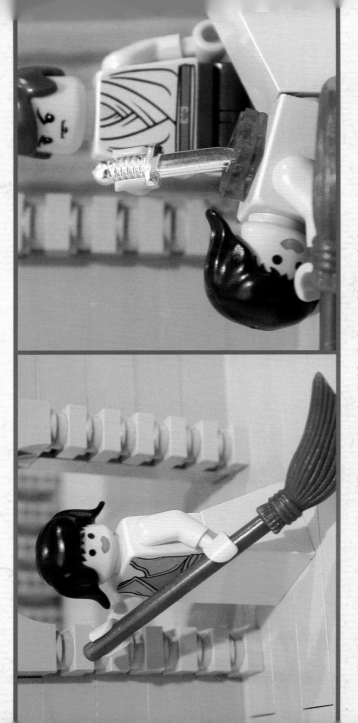

"Remember the Sabbath day and keep it holy.
You shall do no work that day, nor your children, nor your slaves, nor your animals.
Anyone who works on the Sabbath day must be put to death."

Ex 20:8, 31:15

"Honor your father and your mother.
Anyone who strikes their father or mother must be put to death.
Anyone who curses their father or mother must be put to death."

Ex 20:12, 21:15, 17

135

"You shall not kill.
Anyone who strikes a man and kills him must be put to death."

Ex 20:13, 21:12

136

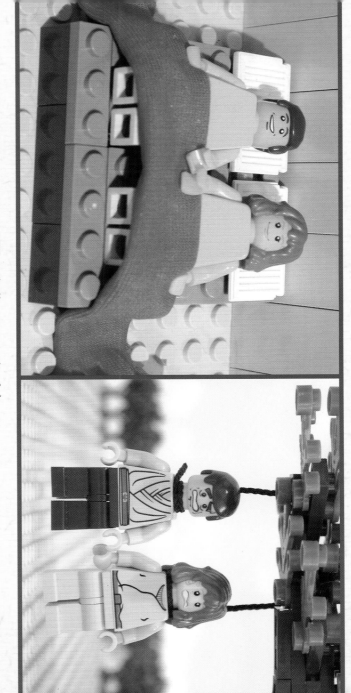

"You shall not commit adultery.
If a man commits adultery with another man's wife,
both the man and the woman must be put to death."

Ex 20:14, Lv 20:10

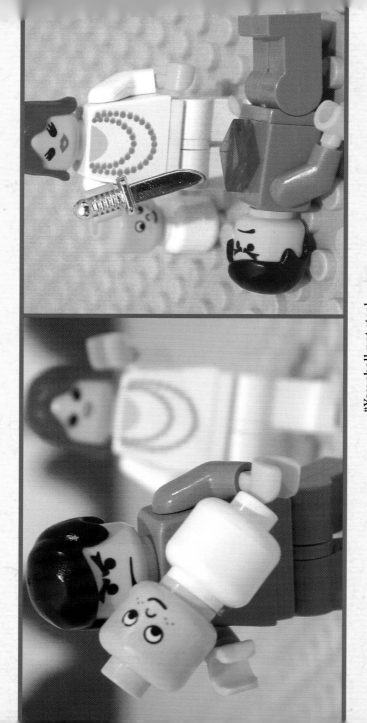

"You shall not steal.
Anyone who steals another person must be put to death."

Ex 20:15, 21:16

"You shall not give false testimony against your neighbor."

Ex 20:16

"You shall not desire your neighbor's house, nor his wife, his male or female slaves, his ox, his donkey, or any of his possessions."

Ex 20:17

The End

The Golden Calf

Then Moses went up the mountain,
and there he stayed for forty days and forty nights.

Ex 24:18

142

When the people saw that Moses was taking a long time to come down from the mountain, they gathered around Aaron and said to him, "Come, make us a god to lead us. For we do not know what has become of Moses, the man who brought us out of Egypt."

Ex 32:1

143

Aaron said to them, "Take off the gold rings in the ears of your wives and your sons and daughters, and bring them to me."

Ex 32:2

144

He took what they gave him and then melted it down.

Ex 32:4

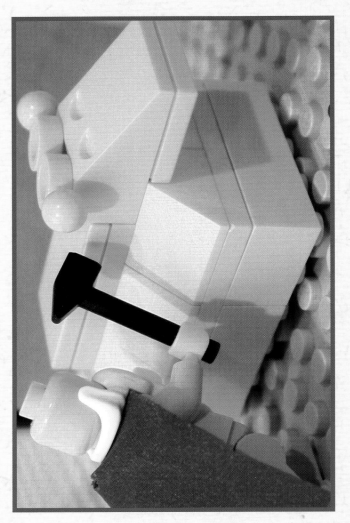

And shaped it into the form of a calf.

Ex 32:4

Then the people said, "Israel, this is your god who brought you up out of Egypt."

Ex 32:4

147

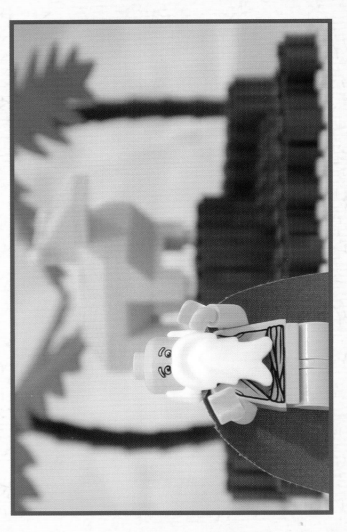

Seeing this, Aaron built an altar before the calf and announced,
"Tomorrow will be a feast to the God of Israel!"

Ex 32:5

And so early the next morning the people sacrificed
burnt offerings and brought peace offerings.

Ex 32:6

The people sat down to eat and to drink and then got up to play.

Ex 32:6

When God had finished speaking to Moses on Mount Sinai,

he gave him the two stone tablets of the Testimony,

inscribed on both sides, front and back.

The tablets were the work of God, and the writing on them was God's writing.

Ex 31:18, 32:16

Moses turned and came down from the mountain
with the two tablets of the Testimony in his hands.

Ex 32:15

When he approached the camp, he saw the calf and the people dancing.

Ex 32:19

153

And Moses burned hot with anger.

Ex 32:19

154

He threw down the tablets from his hands,
smashing them at the base of the mountain.

Ex 32:19

155

He took the calf they had made and burnt it with fire.

Ex 32:20

And he ground it into powder.

Ex 32:20

Then he scattered the powder on the water and made the Israelites drink it.

Ex 32:20

158

When Moses saw that the people were out of control,
he stood at the entrance of the camp and said,
"Whoever is for the God of Israel, come to me!"

Ex 32:25–26

159

All those from the tribe of Levi gathered to him, and Moses said to them, "Each of you take your sword and go up and down the camp from gate to gate, slaughtering your brothers, your friends, and your neighbors."

Ex 32:26–27

The Levites did as Moses ordered.

Ex 32:28

And about three thousand of the people perished that day.

Ex 32:28

The End

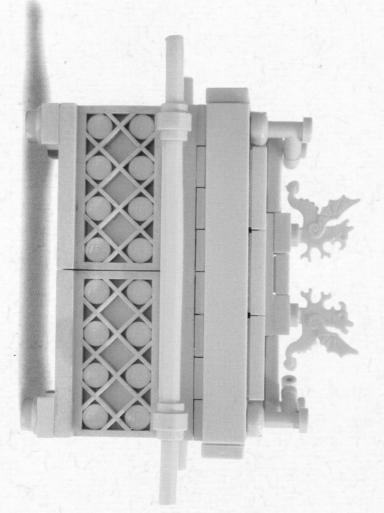

The Ark of the Covenant

God spoke to Moses and said,

"Make me a sanctuary so I can dwell among the people.

You must make it all according to the designs for the Dwelling,

which I shall now show you."

Ex 25:1, 8–9

"Make me an ark of acacia wood.
Overlay it with pure gold, both inside and out. Cast four gold rings
and fix them to the four supports. Make poles of acacia wood and overlay them
with gold and pass them through the rings for carrying it."

Ex 25:10–14

"Make a cover of pure gold, and make two winged creatures out of hammered gold, and put them at either end of the cover."

Ex 25:17–18

"The winged creatures must have their wings spread upward and be facing each other. There above the cover, between the two winged creatures, I will come to meet you, and I shall give you all my commands for the Israelites."

Ex 25:20, 22

167

"Inside the ark you will put the Testimony I will give you."

Ex 25:21

All the work for the Dwelling was done exactly as God had ordered Moses, and the Dwelling was erected on the first day of the first month of the second year.

Ex 39:32, 40:17

Then the cloud covered the Tent of Meeting, and the glory of God filled the Dwelling.

Ex 40:34

170

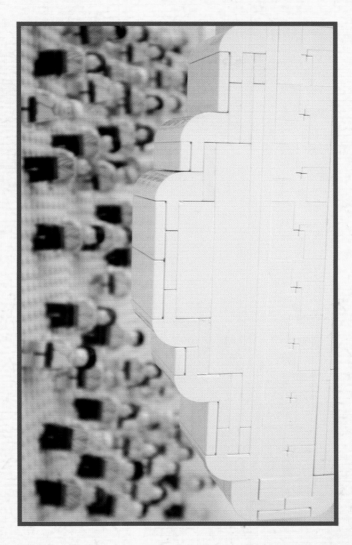

Throughout their journeys, whenever the cloud rose from the Dwelling,
the Israelites would move onward.

Ex 40:36-37

If the cloud did not rise, they would not move on until the day it rose up.

Ex 40:37

And at night there was fire inside the cloud for the whole house of Israel to see throughout their travels.

Ex 40:38

The End

173

"The Reverend" Brendan Powell Smith